Welcome to
I Spy Easter

This book
belongs to:

_____

I Spy with my little eye
Something beginning with...

B

I spied a

Bee

I Spy with my little eye
Something beginning with...

C

I spied a

Chocolate

I spied a

Duckling

I Spy with my little eye
Something beginning with...

E

I spied an

Easter Egg

I Spy with my little eye Something beginning with...

I spied a

Flower

I Spy with my little eye
Something beginning with...

G

I Spy with my little eye
Something beginning with...

H

I spied a

Hat

I Spy with my little eye
Something beginning with...

I spied an

Ice cream

I Spy with my little eye
Something beginning with...

I Spy with my little eye
Something beginning with...

K

I spied a

Kangaroo

I Spy with my little eye
Something beginning with...

I spied a

Lamb

I Spy with my little eye
Something beginning with...

I Spy with my little eye Something beginning with...

I spied a

Nest

I Spy with my little eye Something beginning with...

I spied an

Orange

I Spy with my little eye
Something beginning with...

I spied a

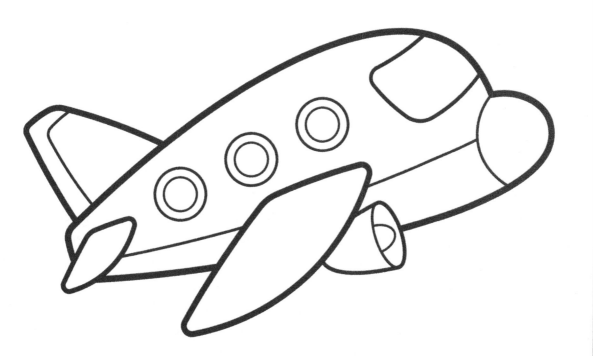

Plane

I Spy with my little eye
Something beginning with...

Q

I spied a

Quail

I Spy with my little eye
Something beginning with...

I spied a

Rabbit

I Spy with my little eye
Something beginning with...

I spied a

Sun

I Spy with my little eye
Something beginning with...

I spied a

Tomb

I Spy with my little eye
Something beginning with...

U

I spied an

Umbrella

I Spy with my little eye Something beginning with...

I spied a

Vase

I Spy with my little eye
Something beginning with...

W

I spied a

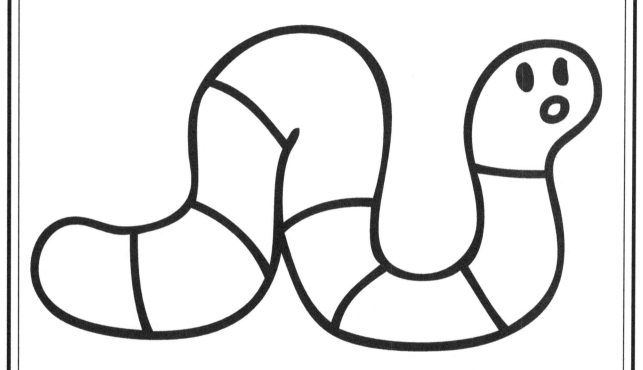

Worm

I Spy with my little eye
Something beginning with...

I Spy with my little eye
Something beginning with...

I spied an

Yacht

I Spy with my little eye
Something beggining with...

I spied a

Zebra

I Spy with my little eye
1 Easter Bunny...

I spied 1 Easter Bunny

I Spy with my little eye
2 Easter Eggs...

I spied 2 Easter Eggs

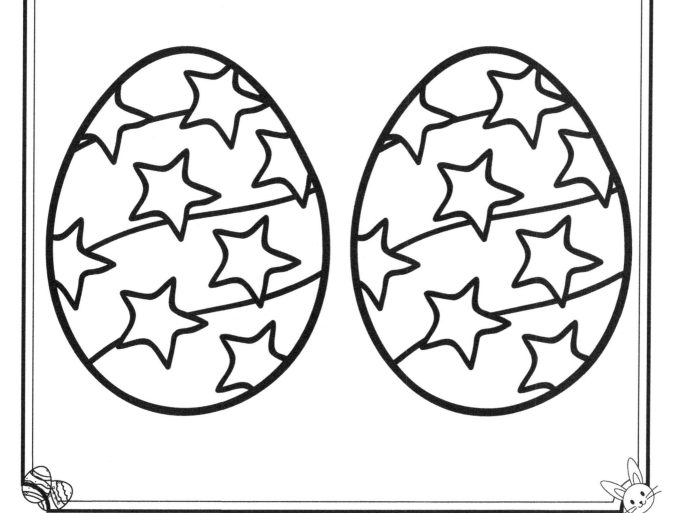

I Spy with my little eye
3 Lambs

I spied 3 Lambs

I Spy with my little eye
4 Flowers

I spied 4 Flowers

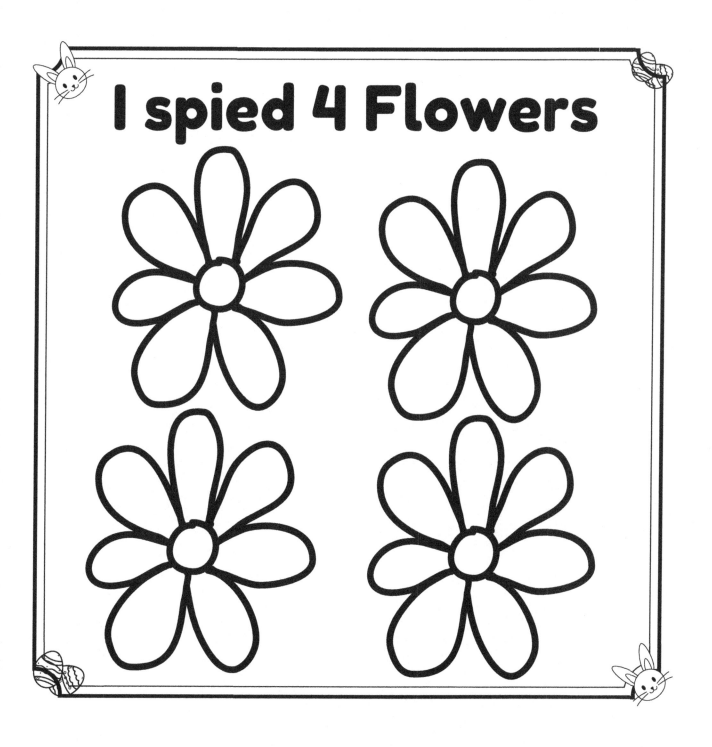

I Spy with my little eye
5 Butterflies

I spied 5 Butterflies

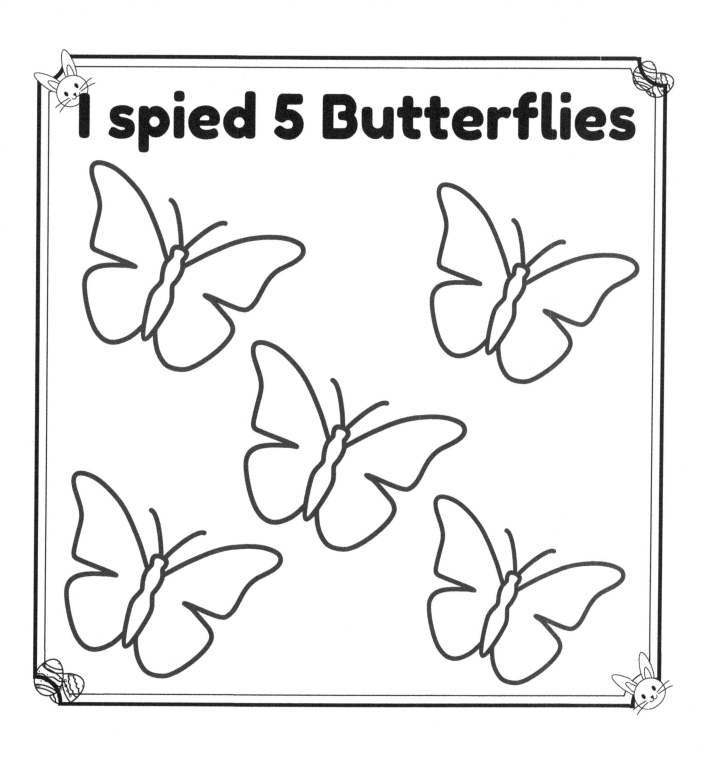

I Spy with my little eye
6 Ladybugs

I spied 6 Ladybugs

I Spy with my little eye
7 Ducklings

I spied 7 Ducklings

I Spy with my little eye
8 Easter Baskets

I spied 8 Easter Baskets

I Spy with my little eye
9 Gifts

I spied 9 Gifts

I Spy with my little eye
10 Bees

I spied 10 Bees

Made in the USA
Coppell, TX
25 March 2024

30529818R00083